BRENT LIBRARIES

Please return/renew this item
by the last date shown.
Books may also be renewed by
phone or online.
Tel: 0333 370 4700
On-line www.brent.gov.uk/libraryservice

911 20000541722

1

This book has been created to entertain and educate young minds and is packed with information and trivia and lots of authentic images that bring the topic alive.

TABLE OF CONTENTS

Introduction to World War One

THE EUROPEAN SITUATION

When it comes to the First World War, there have been a lot of very large and dusty history books written to explain why it happened. When it happened is easier to explain, but if you look at the reasons for long enough you will probably get a headache and come to the conclusion that it is all too complicated and too silly to explain.

However, tension had been growing in Europe for quite some time before the war began. This tension is not between the ordinary people of each country who got along just fine, but between the ruling classes, who are all related through cross-breeding. It is possible that because of this cross-breeding that the ruling classes are slightly mad, but that's another story.

The German rulers are jealous of the British Empire and want a bigger German Empire. The Russian Tsar thinks that a war might make his people more patriotic and stop them complaining about him and the lack of any decent food. The French? Well, they are always up for a fight against the Germans, and the British want to stop German domination.

Countries make alliances with each other based on fear and protectionism. This is not real friendship and will eventually lead to everybody getting involved in the biggest scrap of all time (*Yes, we know about the Second World War, but that was later*).

Basically, in World War One (WW1), there are two teams that don't like each other. The Germans captain the Central Powers.

Britain and France captain the Allies.

The two sides don't trust each other, and because of this begin collecting weapons and making threatening noises. It's a lot of hot air, but by 1914, that air has become so hot in Europe that it only needs a tiny spark for the fighting to begin. That spark happens in Bosnia. In Sarajevo, to be precise, and from then on it is only a matter of time before all of the major powers become involved and take sides.

America is late to the game, but when the Americans eventually show up on the side of the Allies, there is only going to be one outcome.

How it all kicks-off

Assassins from a secret society known as the Black Hand (It sounds a bit cheesy these days, but back then it was kind of a cool name) start the path towards war. The Black Hand members are freedom fighters that want to break away from Austria-Hungarian rule.

"How very dare you, I've just washed my hair, and we have both bought new fancy hats"

On June 28, Archduke Ferdinand of Austria and his wife are shot dead in Sarajevo. The Assassin is a Serbian with a bad haircut called Gavrilo Princip. He is a member of the Black Hand ~~Gang.~~

The Austrian Emperor is 84, and Ferdinand would have been the heir to the throne. Ironically, Ferdinand was a peace-loving man, but now that he has been killed, the Austrians are shouting for revenge.

Austria declares war on Serbia and starts the domino effect towards the Great War (Which turns out to be not that great).

Germany wants to help Austria teach those jumped up Serbians a lesson and Russia prepares to help the Serbians because they are allies. France and Russia are allies as well, so France wants to help the Russians give the Austrians a damn good thrashing.

The Germans march through Belgium to attack France. They want to beat the French and then devote the rest of the war to attacking Russia.

The British don't want the Germans so close to their island, so make an excuse that they will fight to keep Belgium neutral. Germany ignores the threat, so Britain declares war.

The USA watches as all of this is going on, with most Americans happy that they are not involved in the madness. President Woodrow Wilson promises to keep America out of the war, but that promise doesn't last very long.

Everybody thinks that it will be over by Christmas and young men rush to get involved. In fact, it is all over by Christmas, but unfortunately, this is Christmas 1918 after millions have been killed.

The Allies: Russia, Serbia, France, the British Empire, Italy, Belgium and the USA (1917)

The Central Powers: Germany, Austria-Hungary, the Ottoman Empire, and Bulgaria

1914

Austrian propaganda against the Serbs: "We will smash you to pieces"

June 28

The Austrians are really angry with the Serbs because they killed Franz Ferdinand, who was the heir to the throne.

The Austrian Press doesn't try to calm everybody down but whips up mass hysteria and the demand for action.

July 23

The Austrian-Hungarian Empire issues an ultimatum to Serbia. Many politicians in Europe think that the ultimatum is very harsh and has been written so that Serbia cannot possibly accept even to save face. However, the Serbians do agree to most of the ultimatum but refuse the bit that says Austria has to be involved in an internal inquiry into rebellious groups (Like the Black Hand). The Serbs say that this is against their constitution.

July 28

Russian troops marching to war

Despite the Serbs trying to comply with the ultimatum, Austria-Hungary wants revenge and declares war. The tiny state of Serbia is the spark, and the resulting wildfire will eventually spread around the planet. Russia starts mobilizing its troops to help Serbia.

August 1

Germany declares war on Russia because it is mobilizing its troops against Austria

August 3

Germany declares war on France for being Russia's friend

August 4

The Germans are allies of Austria and want to knock out France very quickly. They attack through Belgium, and this wakes up the British, who declare war on Germany.

The German Kaiser (King) is not the brightest lamp in the street but makes up for his stupidity with aggression.

August 23

The first big battle of the war takes place. The Battle of Tannenberg

Russia v Germany

This is a massive victory for the Germans. The Russians have a bigger army, but the Germans are better trained and equipped.

September 5

In the West, the Germans continue to advance until they are stopped at the Battle of Marne by the French.

That's the end of speedy advances, and both sides dig holes in the ground, pull tongues, and shoot at each other for the next four years.

The holes are called trenches, and to live there is your worst nightmare. Luckily, for the British Generals, they get to live in French chateaus (castles) well away from the action. They have to put up with having fewer servants, but the French wine is excellent.

The Americans watch in awe at what is happening. Yet more British men rush to join the Army. They are afraid that the fighting will all be over by Christmas. In Britain, the war propaganda begins churning out stuff about being a patriot and the glory of fighting, even though there is not much glory in living in a hole in the ground. Women call men cowards who don't want to defend their wives, mothers, and children from the devilish Germans. That's the way war works. The leaders need to portray the enemy as evil, whereas in fact, the soldiers on all sides share the same values—the love of country, love of family, and loyalty to friends. In war, things get messed up, and the newspapers don't help that much by stirring up bad emotions. War brings out the dark side of people, and sells newspapers. Some people are going to get very rich out of this war and it is not going to be any of the soldiers who do the fighting.

December

The soldiers stop fighting for Christmas. The Germans and the British exchange gifts and play soccer. Being nice to one another is frowned upon by the commanders, and the troops are told not to let it happen again and ordered to keep on killing each other, which is what they do.

The Brits call their young men to the ~~glorious~~ ridiculous war

Weird but True

If you think that fake news is a new thing, then think again. Back then, it was important that ordinary people hated the enemy, so the press spread rumors.

In Germany, there is a composer called Ernst Lissauer, who wrote a hymn of hate against the English. Germans would greet each other in the street by saying, "God punish England."

Meanwhile, the British believe that the Germans melt down their own dead soldiers into grease, and German music is banned.

World War One is the first war to use planes. In the beginning, the planes would fly over enemy lines and take pictures or drop bombs. After a while, the opposing Army would send up their own planes, and this starts modern-day aerial combat or dogfighting.

The Germans will soon learn that sending bombers to Britain is a good way to strike fear into the British population.

The early planes carry machine guns, but they are every bit as dangerous to the user as to the enemy. It is possible to shoot off your propeller when you pull the trigger. The scientists came up with a way of stopping this. A timing apparatus makes it possible for the bullets to fire through the gaps in the propeller as it is turning. However, like all modern inventions, they sometimes don't work.

In 1915, the war begins to get serious as people realize that Christmas has gone and people are still fighting. This is the year of total war when battles are fought out of slits in the ground called trenches. More countries get involved, and the scientists are trying to think of even more deadly weapons to kill and injure people in nasty ways.

The British start looting German shops in London and attacking anybody with a foreign accent. The Germans are not much better, and both countries set up prisoner of war camps for Germans living in Britain and British people living in Germany. There are rumors everywhere about spies. Most of the rumors are false.

January 19

Zeppelins are used for the first time to bomb Britain on the 19th of January. Two zeppelins bomb coastal towns and kill four people.

The British civilian population is scared, and rumors are in circulation. Germans living in England are thought to be helping the zeppelins find targets by shining car headlights into the sky.

It is even thought that there is a zeppelin base in the English Lake District.

February 2

The German plan is simple. Britain is an island and is supplied

with lots of stuff by ships. Surround the island with submarines and

sink the supply ships and the British will soon be eating cats, spiders, and tree bark. It's a good plan in theory, but…Well, let's leave the sinking of the Lusitania until later.

Gas attack or conga line? Can you guess?

March

With men scrambling to get to the trenches, the Government of Britain wants women to start doing war work to help the cause. Lots of women are up for it and stream into factories and workplaces. In Russia, women are also employed in the Army to fight.

This carries on during the revolution.

April 25

Australian soldiers at Gallipoli: "Where did you say we are?"

The Allies attack the Ottoman Empire (Turkey), and the Battle of Gallipoli begins. This battle is going to last for months and will end in defeat for the Allies. The Allies think that the Turks will be easy to defeat, but they are so wrong. Gallipoli is one of the bloodiest battles of the war, and the Turkish troops defend their homeland like heroes. Most of the attacking allied troops have never even heard of

Gallipoli before they landed on the beaches. Most never make it off the beaches. The best-executed part of this operation by the allies is the retreat.

The Allied attack force consists of British, French, Australian, and New Zealand troops.

After eight months and a quarter of a million casualties, the commanders of the Allied forces decide that the attack hadn't been such a good idea after all and abandon the campaign.

In Turkey, this is considered to be a great victory.

In Britain, the war cabinet says "Oops" and carry on with the war as if nothing has happened. For them, nothing had, but in Britain and the Empire, many dads, sons, and brothers are never going to come home.

Future British Prime Minister of Britain, Winston Churchill, resigns over the Gallipoli disaster and heads for the trenches to fight like a man. He thinks his political career is over, but what does he know!

The Western Front is still deadlocked in April, but the Germans release a deadly weapon against the French. They launch about 150 tons of chlorine gas, and the French troops are devastated by the attack.

May 7

The Lusitania is sent to the bottom of the ocean by a German submarine.

Onboard were 128 American passengers.

There is outrage in America. Could the USA enter the war? Not yet, but there is talk about the possibility.

President Wilson remains calm.

The Lusitania is identified by U-boat U-20 and takes around 18 minutes to sink after the torpedo hit it.

The Lusitania is about 11 miles off the Irish Coast. There are 1,192 deaths and 761 survivors.

German U-boat pens: One of these sent the Lusitania to the bottom. Can you see which one?

August

There is a shortage of food in Europe, and the price goes up. Germany is especially hit, and people start eating the strangest meals.

The British Navy is king of the seas and oceans. Soon after the war begins, the Navy starts to blockade Germany in a bid to starve the population. The Germans do the same to Britain using submarines, which is a lot sneakier.

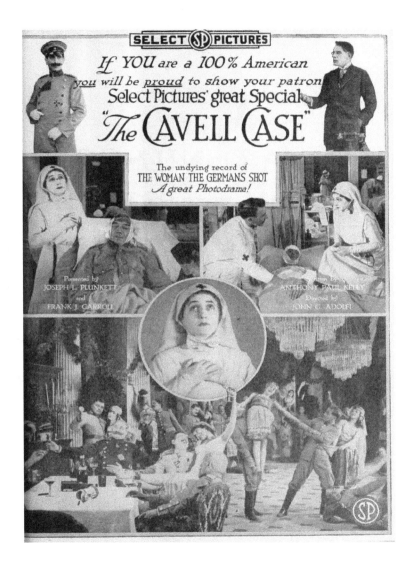

The woman those spiteful Germans shot

British Nurse, Edith Cavell, saves the lives of many wounded

soldiers in German-occupied Belgium. For Edith, it doesn't matter which side they are on; however, she is accused of treason by the Germans and shot. The world is furious, and just about everybody condemns the Germans.

October 14

Bulgaria declares war on Serbia and enters the war.

Curious but True

The British try to get the Americans to join in the war by planting fake stories in American newspapers.

Some soldiers are as young as 12 and join the Army to get away from their dreary lives. They are in search of excitement but are in for a shock when they arrive in the trenches.

Trench war is mostly dull, with both sides stuck in the mud.

Life in the trenches leads to diseases that can kill and are just as deadly as a bullet.

You know life is not that great when you start to envy the rats that live in the trench with you.

Are you sure this is the way?

Going 'over the top' means attacking the enemy's trench. The tactic is thought up by some bright spark back in the War Office. The space between the two trenches is called no man's land and is basically a killing area.

The Rules of the Game

1 Leave the trench when the whistle blows

2 Walk very slowly towards the enemy trench

3 Try to avoid the thousands of machine gun bullets being fired at you.

4 Scramble over dead bodies of your mates, avoid the mud, and the bomb craters and cut the barbed wire.

5 If you reach the enemy trench (well done, you). Now, start fighting with the Germans hand-to-hand.

6 Oh yes, I nearly forgot. If you don't climb out of the trench when the whistle blows, then an officer will shoot you with his pistol.

Got all of that! Off you jolly-well go…

Some soldiers try to get out of their duties by rubbing explosive called cordite into their eyes. Cordite, if rubbed into the eyes, gives the same symptoms as the flu. Unfortunately, the officers soon catch on to the trick.

A World War One Joke

These jokes are often brutal and poked fun at the dangers of war.

The British came up with a plan to kill more Germans. They decided that the most popular name in Germany was Hans.

An English soldier called out from his trench. "Hans!" A German's head popped up and said, "Ja?"

BOOM… The German was shot dead.

The day after, the British soldier shouted again. "Hans!"

A German's head popped up and said, "Ja?"

BOOM… The German was shot dead.

This carried on for weeks, and then the Germans caught on and decided to do the same thing back. They agreed that the most popular English name was George.

The next day, a German soldier shouted, "George!"

An English soldier shouted back. "Hans, is that you?"

A German's head popped up and said, "Ja?"

BOOM… The German was shot dead.

1916

In January, the British introduce conscription. This means that rather than volunteer to fight for King and Country, you are forced to whether you like it or not. If you don't go, the girls will give you a white feather and say that you aren't a real man. For the millions of men that had joined the Army to prove their manhood, 1916, gave them the perfect opportunity. The Battle of the Somme.

February 21

Are we there yet? French cavalry head towards Verdun

The Germans and the French fight out the longest battle of the war. The battle of Verdun takes place in the North East of France. The fighting lasts until December and ends with a French victory.

There are 800,000 casualties at this battle, and over 70 percent are caused by artillery fire from big guns. The Germans fire more than two million shells.

May 31

There is fun at sea in May as the mighty Royal Navy take on the proud German fleet.

The Battle of Jutland is a close run thing, and both sides claim victory.

However, the German Navy never try to fight the British Navy again after Jutland, so actions speak louder than words.

The outcome of this battle was more than likely a moral victory to Germany, but the superior numbers of British Warships and sailors meant that the British could afford the losses more than the Germans. Germany in this war and the next would use their submarines to try to starve the British into submission. At times they almost succeed.

Damaged but not sunk: the German Battlecruiser SMS Seydlitz

July 1

It's summer and time to ruin it with the Battle of the Somme. The fighting takes place near the River Somme and lasts until November. There is a saying going around that the

British troops heading for the Somme

British troops are, 'Lions led by Donkeys,' and the Somme is a perfect example of this.

The plan is simple enough. Pound the Germans with shells for a very, very, very long time, and then attack. Johnny German will be too stunned or too dead to fight back. Well, wouldn't he?

Er… No, not really. The Germans took shelter underground, played on their iPhones (I know) until the bombing ceases. They came out and manned their guns and mowed down the British as they strolled towards them.

In Theory

After eight days of bombardment, the commanders, who are stationed well behind the front-line trenches, are told that it has not been a success.

The commanders think about it for a bit and say, "Attack."

Thousands of British troops do what they have been ordered to do. They do their duty and attack.

Result: The worst day in the history of British military action. There are 60,000 casualties and 20,000 killed. Not to be put off by a few dead bodies, the British troops and their allies keep on attacking. In fact, they attack until November and gain about seven miles. The Allies have 623,000 casualties and the Germans, 500,000.

Interesting facts about the battle

Because many British men join up as friends from the same towns; when they are killed the towns lose most of their men.

Tanks are used in battle for the first time on the Somme

For every mile gained, nearly 90,000 men were lost

"Somehow, I thought that a tank would be much bigger"

Thankfully, it snows in November, so the campaign comes to a halt.

Strange but true

The Battle of the Somme puts an end to 'Pals Battalions.' The British thought that if neighbors, friends, and workmates from a town or village joined the Army together, they were more likely to volunteer. Thus, we see, in some instances, nearly all of the young men of a town in one battalion. The colossal loss of life at the Somme devastates communities. The army leaders gradually disperse people from the same community to other battalions, so this will never happen again.

British General Sir Henry Rawlinson advises troops to attack enemy trenches by walking in evenly spaced lines. This is, of course, ridiculous. Many of the British officers have only pistols and sticks.

A German corporal from Bavaria is wounded in the leg at the Battle of the Somme. He is lucky to escape death, but the world might have been different if he hadn't. That soldier's name was Hitler. Adolph Hitler. Maybe at the Somme, he vowed to make the British pay for hurting him.

1917

This year is the turning point and is the one in which American troops ride into Europe like the cavalry and save the day. Maybe if they hadn't entered the war, the outcome would have been better for the future. Without the Americans, experts predicted that the whole thing would have come to a standstill, and both sides would have called it a draw.

As it is, the Germans are so worried about America that they actively help the Communist Party (Bolsheviks) in Russia to get rid of the Tsar. The Germans think that without the Tsar, the Russians will call for a truce...Which is what happens. If we could see into the future, maybe we would do things differently. With a communist Russia, the world will be subject to a Cold War between the East and the West for many years.

January

The British intercept a message sent by Germany to Mexico. It isn't to order authentic enchiladas with extra hot sauce, it's asking for help.

The notorious Zimmerman Telegram wants Mexico to attack the USA and promises land and money in return.

The Brits show the telegram to the Americans, and the Americans show the telegram to the American public.

There is an immediate call for war.

February

The Russians rebel against their leader, the Tsar. They are sick of having no food and getting killed by the Germans.

The Russian leader Tsar Nicholas II gives up the throne in March.

April 6

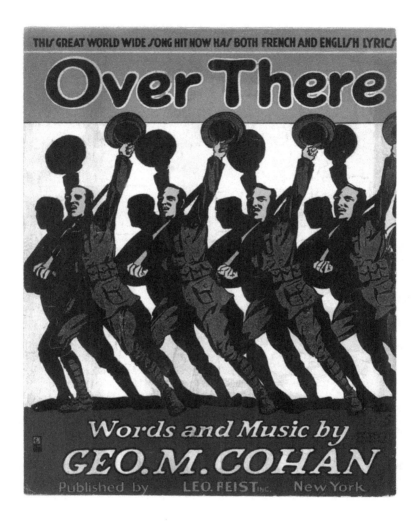

"Where did you say Belgium is?" The Americans didn't really dance their way to the trenches

The USA declares war on Germany. The French troops think that American troops will arrive straight away. When they don't, they start sulking and then rebel against the terrible conditions. Like the Russians, they are sick of getting killed and having no food. They tell their leaders that they hate living in holes in the ground, and don't want to get cut to pieces attacking the horrible Germans anymore.

French leaders don't understand and put down the rebellion. The ring leaders of the rebellion are shot or sent to Devils Island, which is not a very nice prison, as the name implies.

November

Vladimir Lenin and his Bolsheviks (Communists) overthrow the Government of Russia. It doesn't come as a surprise that by Christmas, they have agreed on a peace deal with Germany.

Life in a trench

Hello, my name is Billy Smith, and I come from Grimsby, which is a little town on the east coast of England. I'm 21 years old and live in a trench.

The Army never told me that I would be living in a ditch, and maybe I wouldn't have come if I had known what it would be like. They told us that it would be glorious fighting the Germans and that they were a bad bunch. I met a few of them at Christmas, and they were all a bit like me, only German.

Trench life is very boring most of the time, but that is mixed in with moments of sheer terror.

It's like living on the edge of a cliff with a blindfold on.

The idea that you might die keeps any happy thoughts out of your head.

Living in a trench…Mmm… it's like the worst horror movie that you have ever seen multiplied by ten.

The only good thing is that you don't have to pay for your ticket, but there's no popcorn.

The food here is terrible, and we share it with rats. God, I wish I was a rat!

Le Barbier dans la tranchée

Life doesn't get much better than this! In a trench

They wake us up at dawn, and we eat breakfast. The food is mostly tinned bully beef, bread, and beans with tea that tastes of petrol. We sleep in dugouts cut into the walls of the trench. These are damp, full of insects, flies, lice, and rats.

In the day, we are all given jobs to do, like repairing the trench and filling sandbags. At night, some of us sneak out and fix the barbed wire or shoot at the enemy's trench. We spend a bit of time in a front line trench, a bit of time in the backup trench, and a bit of time resting.

Last winter was so cold; some of the lads suffered from frostbite and had to have toes and fingers cut off. There is also the mud, which sucks you under if you aren't careful. In the summer, there are millions of flies, and let's not talk about the smell, which is obscenely terrible.

The smell is nothing compared to the fear you have all of the time that you will be the next to get hit by a bullet or blown up by a shell. War is not very nice and far from glorious.

1917 WW1 Joke

Sentry: "Halt, who goes there?"

Answer: "Scots Guard."

Sentry: "Pass Scots Guard."

Sentry: "Halt, who goes there?"

Answer: "Irish Guard."

Sentry: "Pass Irish Guard."

Sentry: "Halt, who goes there?"

Answer: "English Guard."

Sentry: "Pass English Guard."

Sentry: "Halt, who goes there?"

Answer: "Mind your god-damn business."

Sentry: "Pass American trooper."

1918

American troops pitching grenades at the Germans for fun

The two teams have been battering each other for three years, but now with the arrival of American troops, the Germans know that unless they do something, and fast, they will be defeated.

The Germans attack the Allies in the spring of 1918. Even though American troops have been arriving, America is not fully prepared for the war. It will take time to get the full might of the USA involved in the bloodshed; the Germans decide to finish the war as quickly as possible.

January/February

Food is in short supply in Britain, and British families are forced to have two meatless days a week. Butter, sugar, and margarine are in short supply, and there are huge queues for food that stretch from one street to another.

In Turkey and Russia, the distribution of food to peasants is almost nonexistent, and people begin to starve. The same is true in Austria-Hungary and Germany. The Germans begin to invent food out of weird ingredients. Thus, to go with fake news, we now have fake food.

Meat is substituted with vegetable steak that is slimy green and made from spinach and turnips.

Coffee is produced by roasting nuts and adding black coal tar.

Bread is made from potatoes and turnip flour, and at desperate times sawdust is added.

This fake food doesn't kill you, it fills up empty stomachs.

For German troops who are fighting, the story is the same. They are sick of eating turnip stew with turnip bread. If the bombs and bullets don't kill you, then the turnips will.

The Germans are hungry, and the will to carry on the war is a lot less in 1918 than in 1914. Like a trench, there is nothing glorious about a turnip.

March 21

The Germans launch a spring offensive, and the plan is to defeat the Allies before American troops arrive in large numbers.

The plan seems to be working, but the Germans are victims of their success.

The further they advance, the more difficult it becomes to supply the front line troops with turnips, and the equipment necessary to win the battle.

In July, with more and more American troops arriving, the German offensive grinds to a halt, and they begin to be pushed back.

July 15

These German prisoners don't look too unhappy to be out of the war

The Second Battle of Marne starts and lasts until August 6.

The Germans are defeated, and all is lost.

More than 85,000 American troops take part in the battle, and suffer heavy losses, like the rest of the Allies and the Germans.

To get some idea of the scale of losses:

- French 95,165 dead or wounded

- Americans 45,807 dead or wounded

- British 16,552 dead or wounded

- Italian 9000 dead or wounded

- Germans 139,000 dead or wounded and 29,367 captured

November 11

Germany agrees on a truce and the fighting stops at 11 am on the 11th day of the 11th month of 1918.

On June 28, 1919, the signing of the Treaty of Versailles by Germany formally brings the war to an end.

Germany owes us all this money for the damage it caused

If the Germans think that they will negotiate a peace agreement with the Allies and then everything will get back to normal; they are wrong.

There is so much hatred and ill-feeling against Germany that the public of France and Britain will not hear of it, and the politicians have to comply if they want to keep their jobs.

Germany is not consulted and not allowed to sit down and negotiate the terms of peace. They are presented with the terms and conditions and told to sign or else.

They are told that they have been very naughty and caused so much damage that they will have to pay for it.

Which of course, they did, and it causes so much hardship in Germany that by the 1930s, they are so angry with Britain and France that they are ready for another fight.

Adolph Hitler survives the Somme and will wreak havoc in 1939

In the 1930s, a young politician (guess who?) told them that they had not lost the war, but that they had been stabbed in the back by Jewish Bankers.

That politician was Adolph Hitler. The man who almost copped it on the Somme. It's funny how things turn out!

Crazy World War One

Canadian troops meet French Tank, but should they address the tank as Monsieur or Madame?

Tanks in the First World War were grouped according to gender. Male tanks had cannons while female tanks had machine guns. The prototype tank was called 'Little Willie.'

The war plan of Germany was called the Schlieffen Plan. It required Germany to defeat the French in six weeks and then attack

Russia. This would avoid a war on two fronts. The plan didn't work out too well!

A lot of British politicians didn't want the country to get involved in the war and didn't care about the Germans attacking France through Belgium.

Russia had an army of over five million. Unfortunately, they were poorly equipped and lacked training. They were soundly beaten by the Germans at the Battle of Tannenberg and never really recovered.

The German submarine fleet numbered 360. They suffered huge losses, and 176 were sunk.

By 1917, there was so much anti-German feeling in Britain that the Royal Family had to change its name from the German-sounding Saxe-Coburg and Gotha to the more English sounding, Windsor.

A conscientious objector is a man who refuses to fight. In Britain, there were 16,000. Some were given non-combatant roles, and others were put in prison.

Did anybody ask the horses if they wanted to fight? They would
have probably said, "Neigh."

At the beginning of the war, soldiers were issued with cloth caps. These looked cute but gave no protection.

Later in the war, they were given steel helmets.

On day one of the Battle of Verdun, 7,000 horses were killed by bullets and bombs. The war claimed the lives of over 8 million horses.

One hundred things you can do with your turnip: Turnip bread, turnip burgers, turnip coffee, turnip tea, turnip sausages….Turnip meatball?

The winter of 1916/17 became known as the 'turnip winter' in Germany. This was because turnips were used to make almost everything. There was turnip stew, turnip bread, turnip meat, and lots more crazy recipes. It is not surprising that Germans were sick of the sight of turnips by the end of the war. Turnip ice cream? Maybe not…

In Germany, the blockade caused famine, hunger, and death amongst the civilian population. Meat was impossible to find, so the population lived on bread…The bread was made from, you've guessed it, turnip flour.

Casualties due to the war were over 37 million.

Over 7 million troops had limbs amputated or suffered horrific injuries.

Between 1914 and 1918, 230 soldiers were killed every hour.

Australian troops suffered the worst, and 65% of them were injured or killed.

The end of World War One marked the end of four empires.

- The Ottoman Empire
- The Austria-Hungarian Empire
- The German Empire
- The Russian Empire

As a result of the war, Estonia, Finland, Lithuania, and Poland emerged as sovereign nations.

Russia made sure that the Tsar would never return to the throne by killing him and his family.

The Treaty of Versailles was signed between Germany and the Allies. Under the terms and conditions, Germany was forced to pay back $31.4 billion for all of the damage it had caused in Europe; by anybody's reasoning, this was very harsh.

The German Army was capped at 100,000, and they were not allowed more than six battleships. Germany was not allowed an air force.

Germany lost 13% of its territory, which didn't sit down too well with its citizens who were living in those territories.

The effect of the Treaty of Versailles would have long-lasting consequences and was written by short-sighted politicians. Germans called the people who signed the document, 'The November Criminals,' and refused to accept the fact that they had lost the war.

French General Ferdinand Foch had some harsh words about the treaty. He said that it wasn't a peace agreement but a 20-year armistice. He was correct, but nobody believed him at the time.

And America? America never signed the Treaty of Versailles.

Fun Quiz about WW1

1 Name one country that was in the Central Powers

2 Name one country that made up the Allies

3 Who was assassinated in Sarajevo on June 28th, 1914?

4 What countries fought in the Battle of Tannenberg?

5 What empire did the Allies attack in the Battle of Gallipoli?

6 Which future Prime Minister of Britain resigned over the disastrous Gallipoli campaign?

7 What Luxury steamship did a German submarine sink on May 7, 1915?

8 What was the name of the British Nurse, accused of treason, who was shot in October 1915 by the Germans?

9 What year did America declare war on Germany?

10 What was the land called between the Allied trenches and the Central Powers?

11 What battle started in July 1916 and lasted until November?

12 What year did the fighting stop in the First World War?

13 What was the name of the peace treaty the ended the First World War?

14What was the name of the German corporal who was wounded at the Battle of the Somme?

15 What was the name of the prototype tank that was made by the British?

Answers to the Fun Quiz

1 Germany, Austria-Hungary, the Ottoman Empire, and Bulgaria.

2 Britain and its Empire, France, Russia, France, Italy, Belgium, and the USA.

3 Archduke Franz Ferdinand of Austria

4 Russia and Germany

5 The Ottoman Empire

6 Winston Churchill

7 The Lusitania

8 Edith Cavell

Other Books by George Joshua

Click Follow, and you will get updates on new publications.

Timelines

Timeline World War One

Other Books in the Pocket History Series

World War Two Facts and Trivia

Weird and Interesting War Facts

The Titanic Story

The American Revolutionary War

World War One Facts and Trivia

The Early American Colonies Explained

The Cold War Explained

Lightning Source UK Ltd.
Milton Keynes UK
UKHW010701021222
413182UK00001B/19